CRITTERS on SHROOMs

THIS BOOK BELONGS TO:

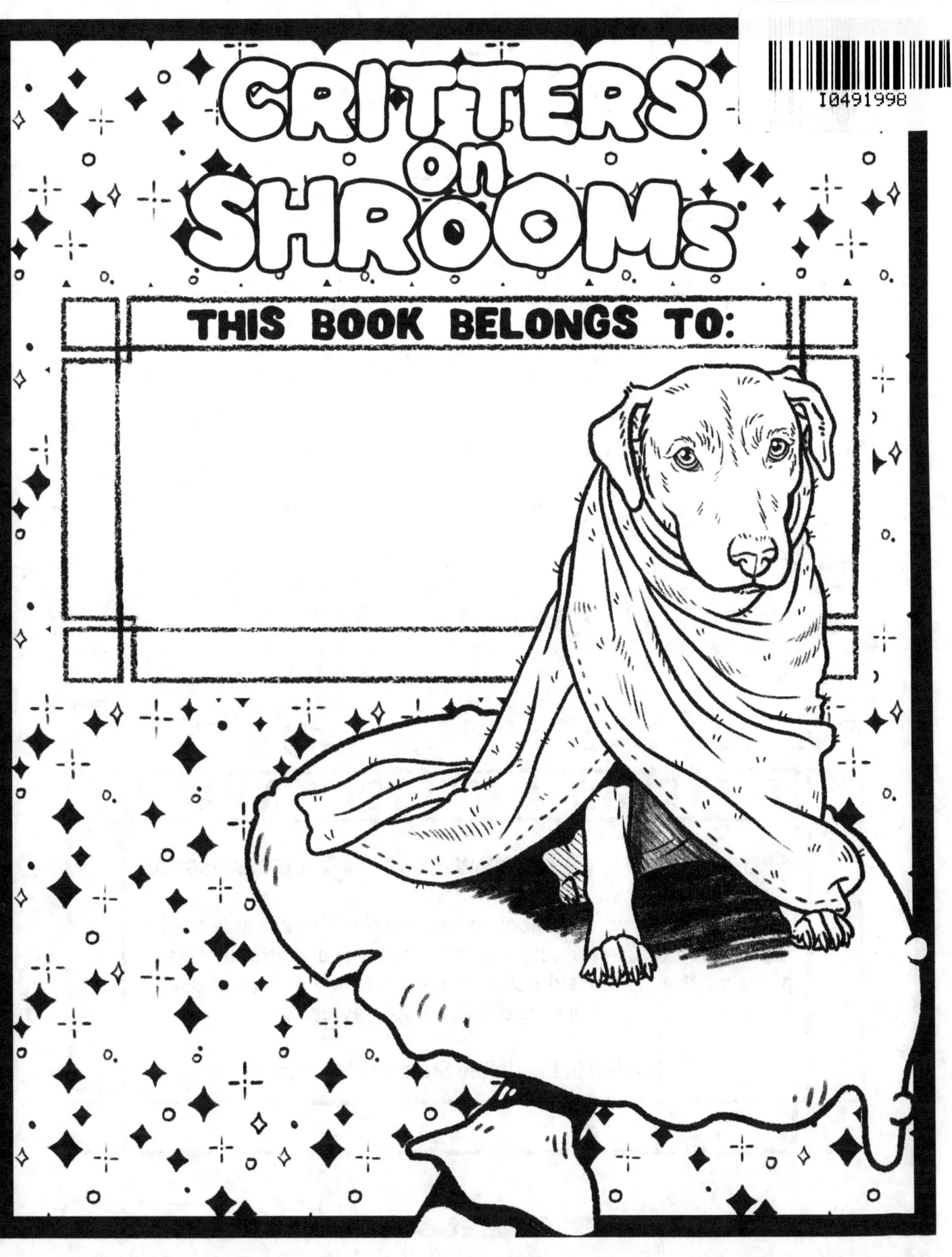

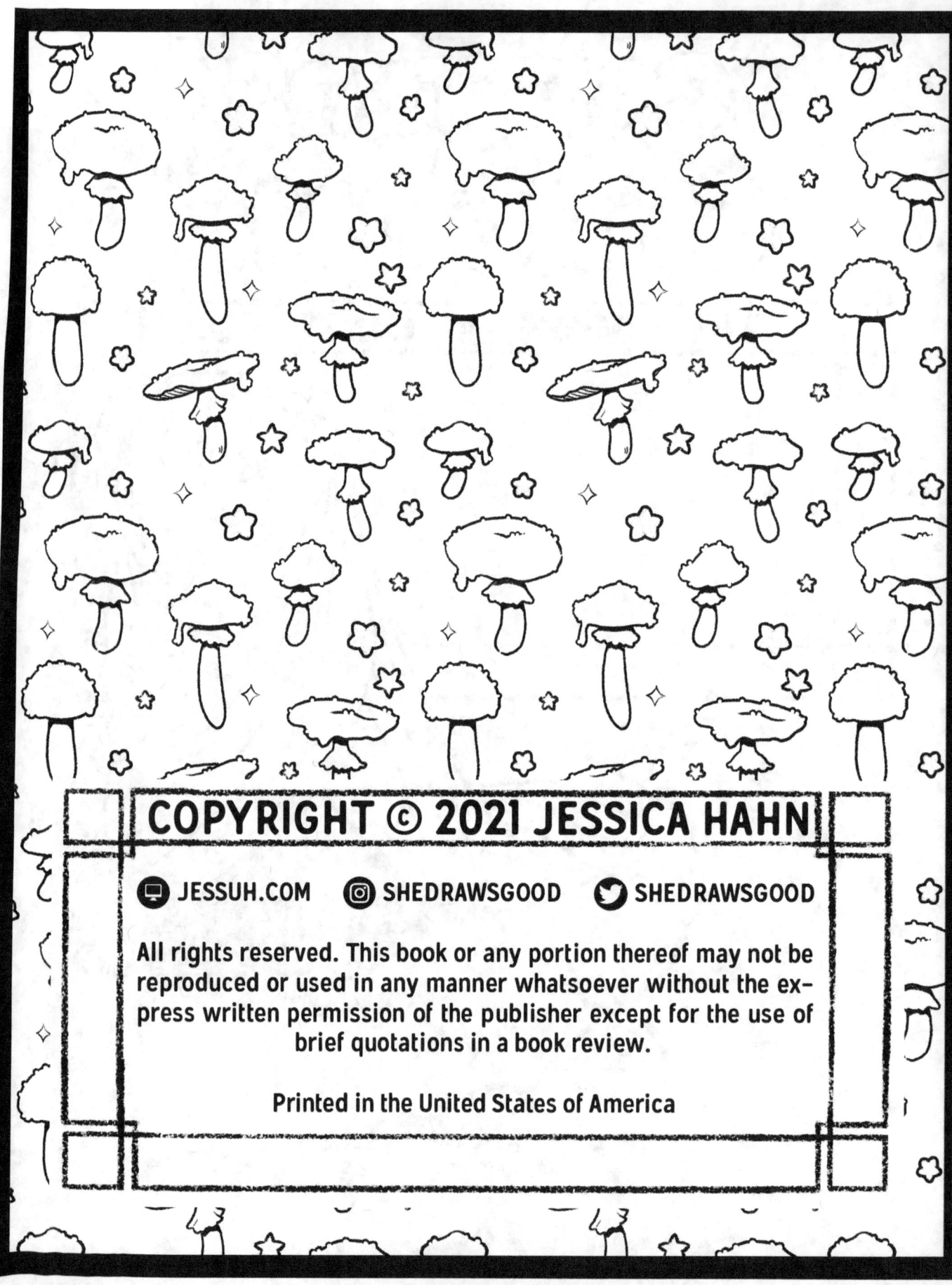

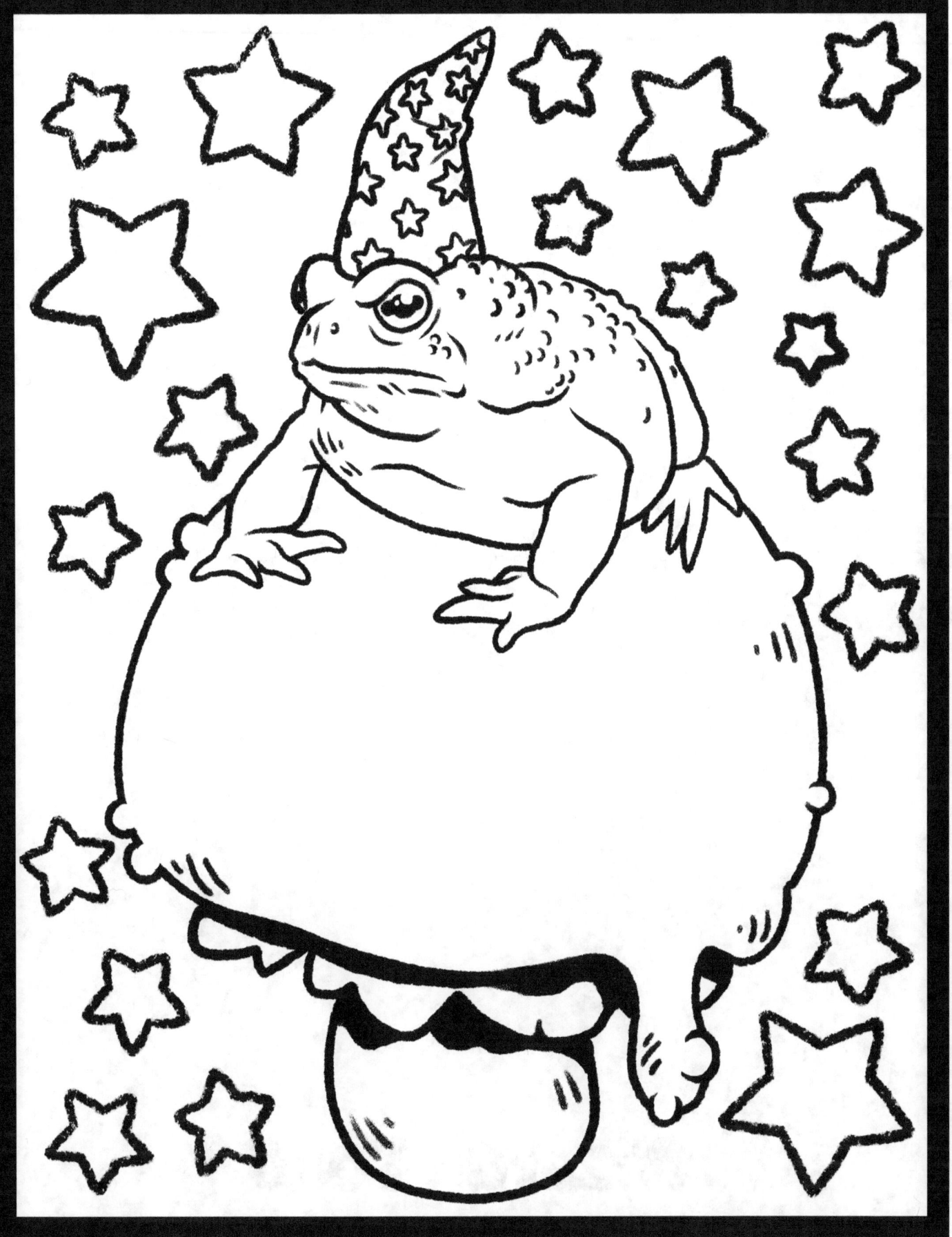

Wizard Toad

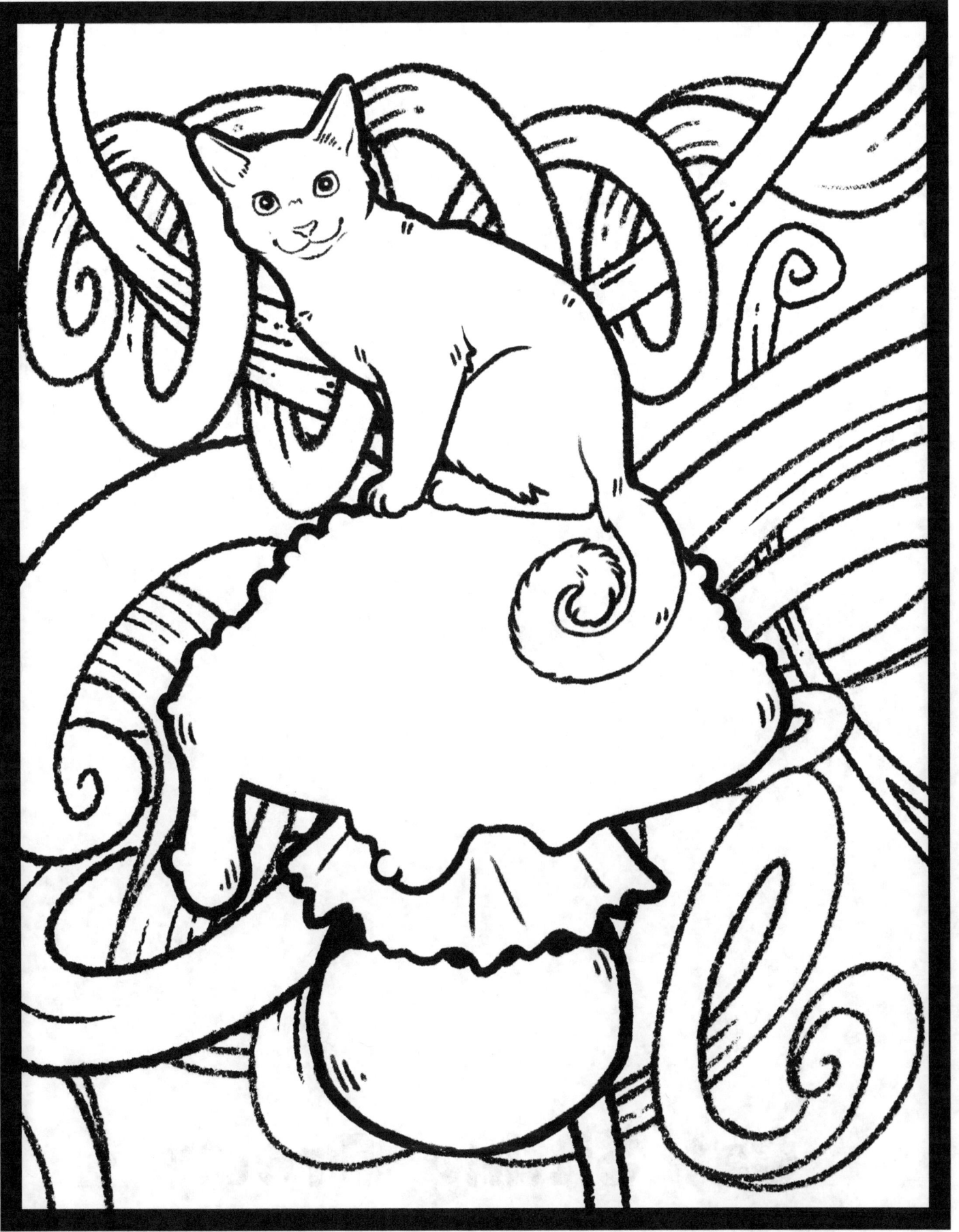

Cat Sitting Pretty

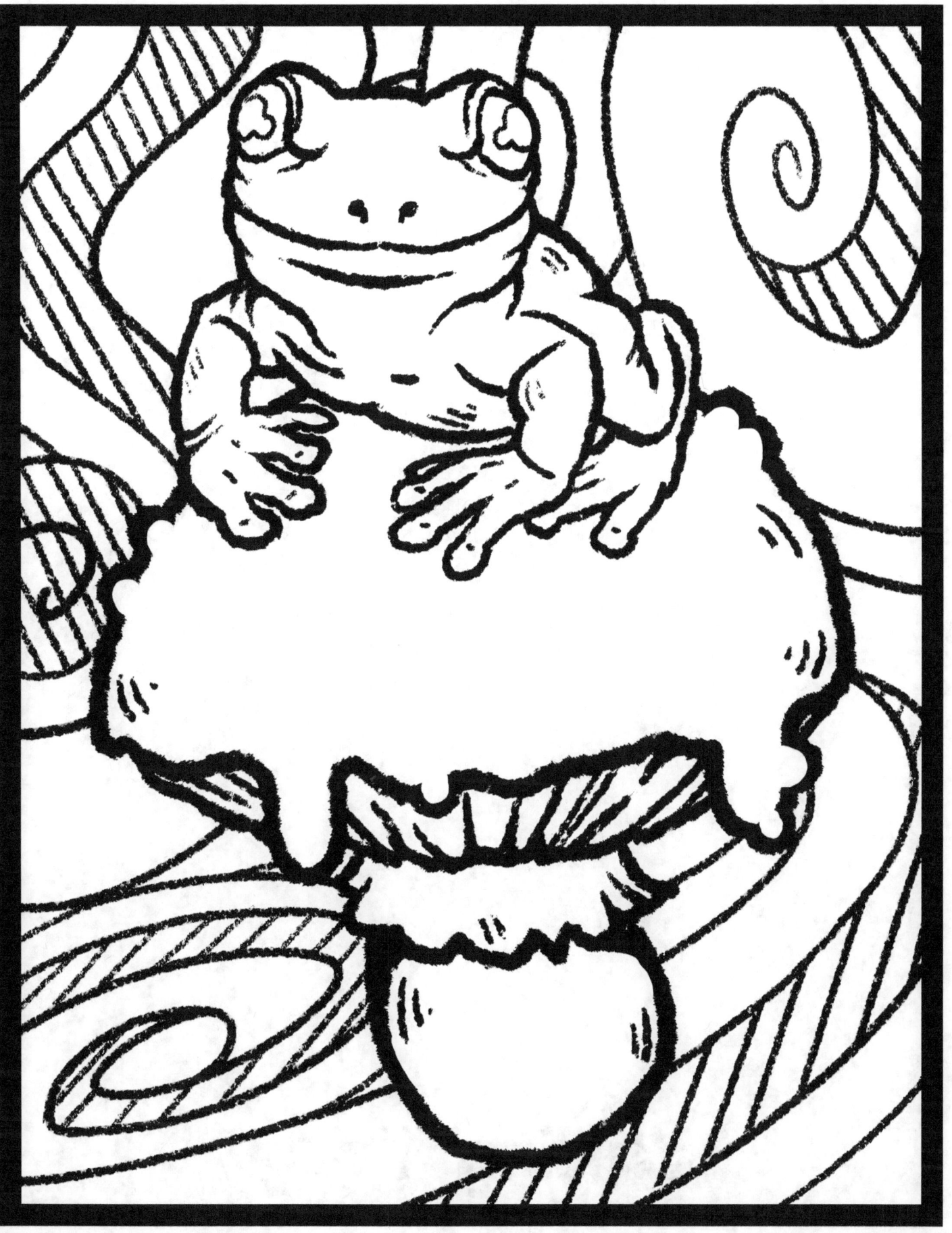

Smiling Frog

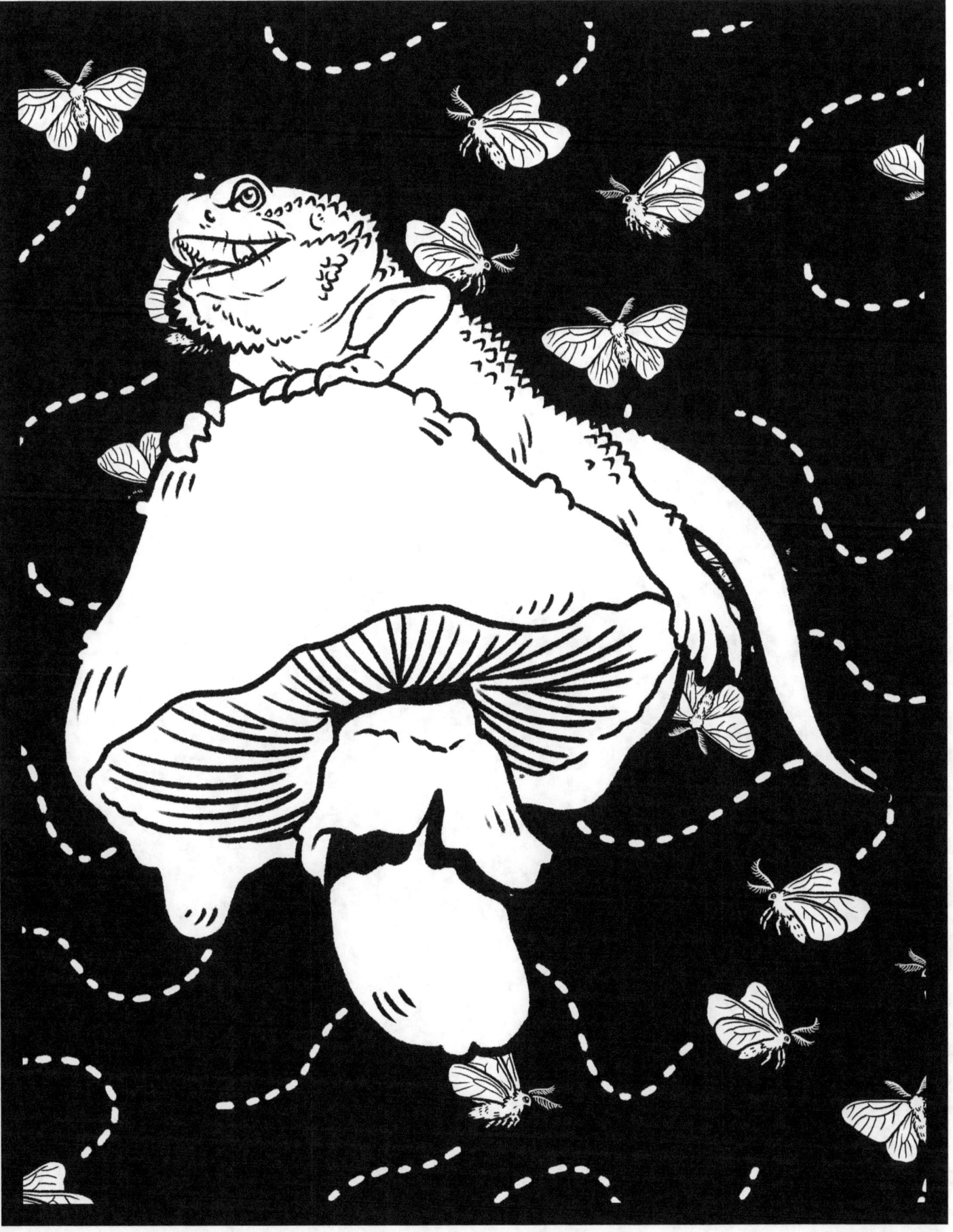

Grumpy Beardie

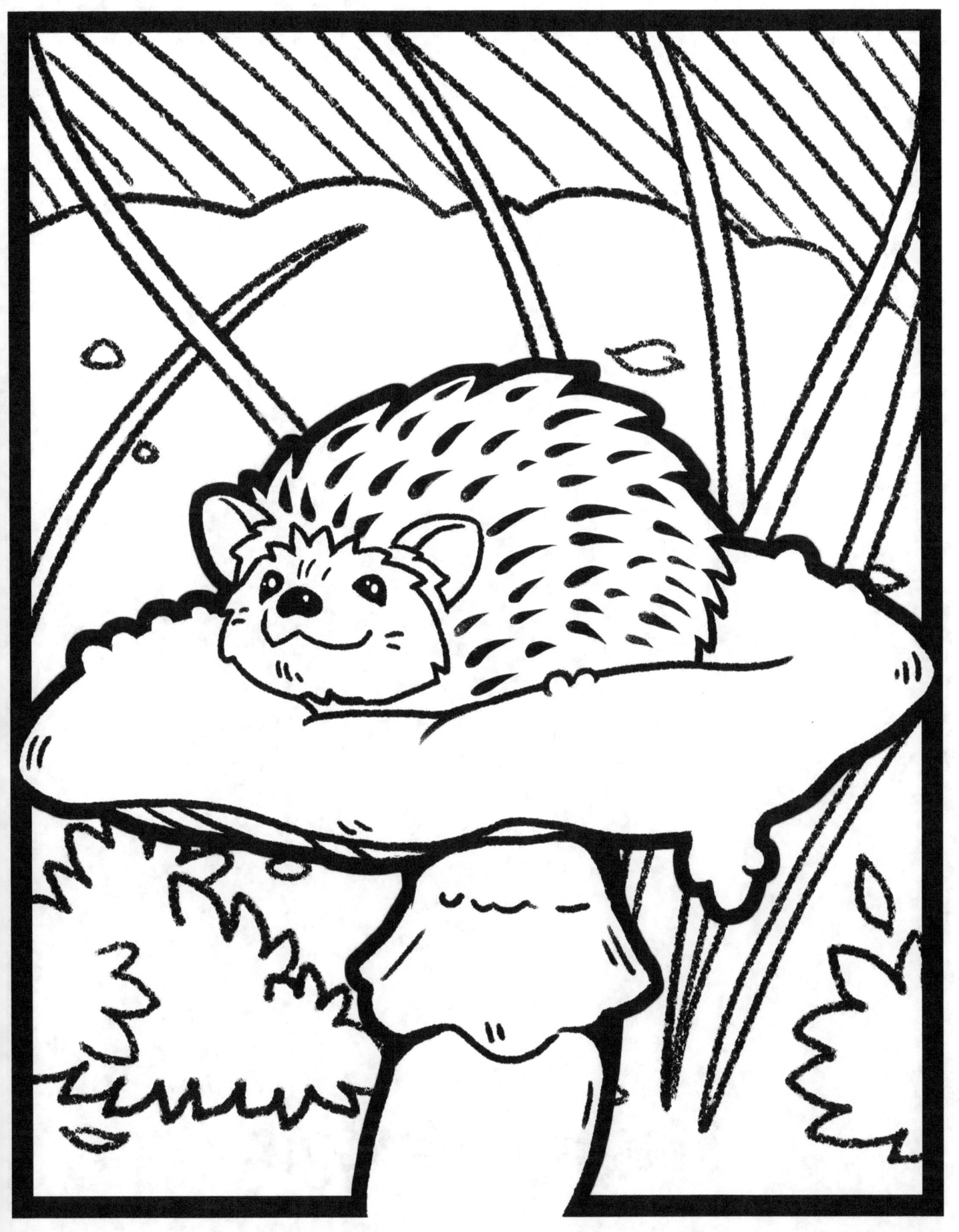

Happy Hedgie

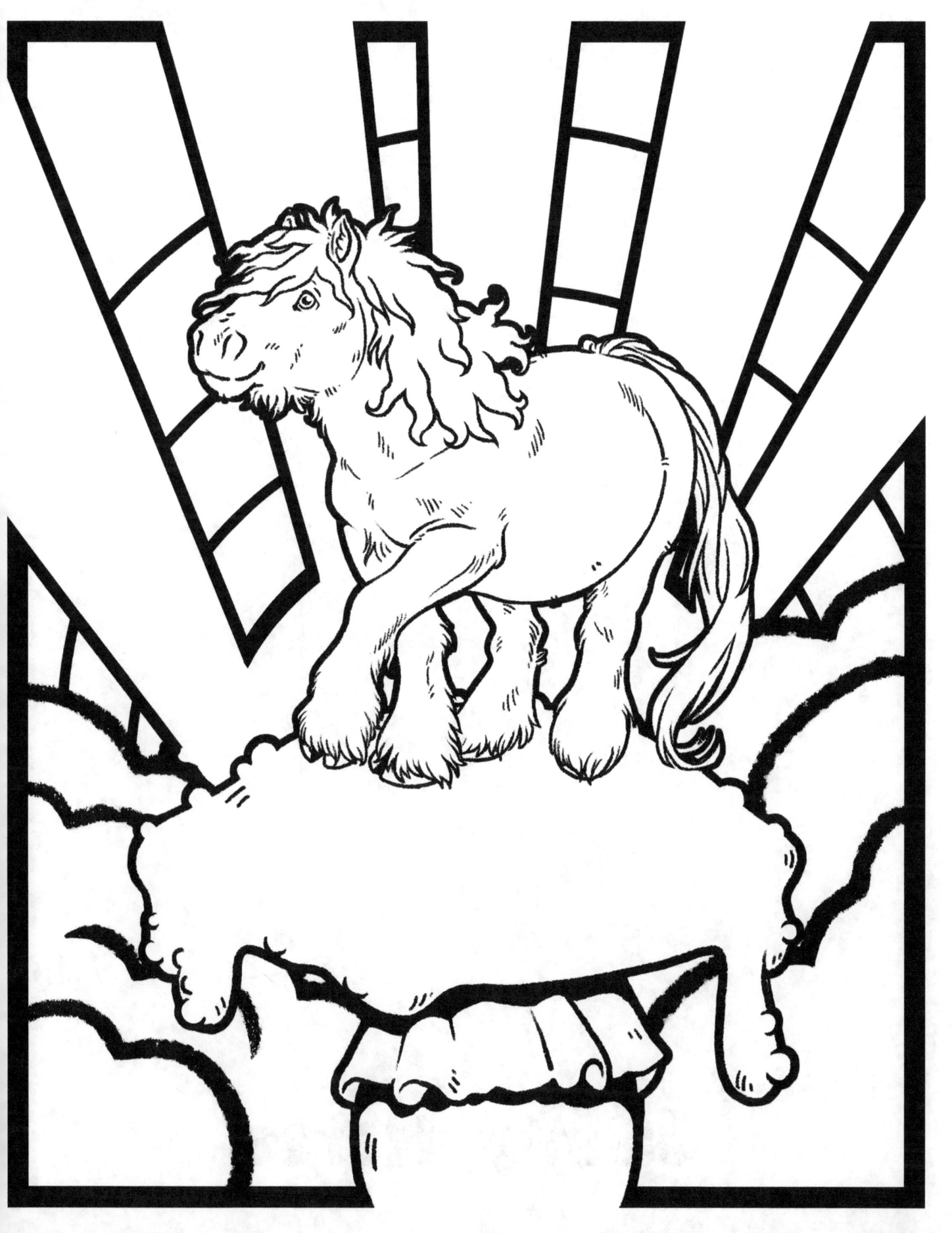

Jaunty Horse

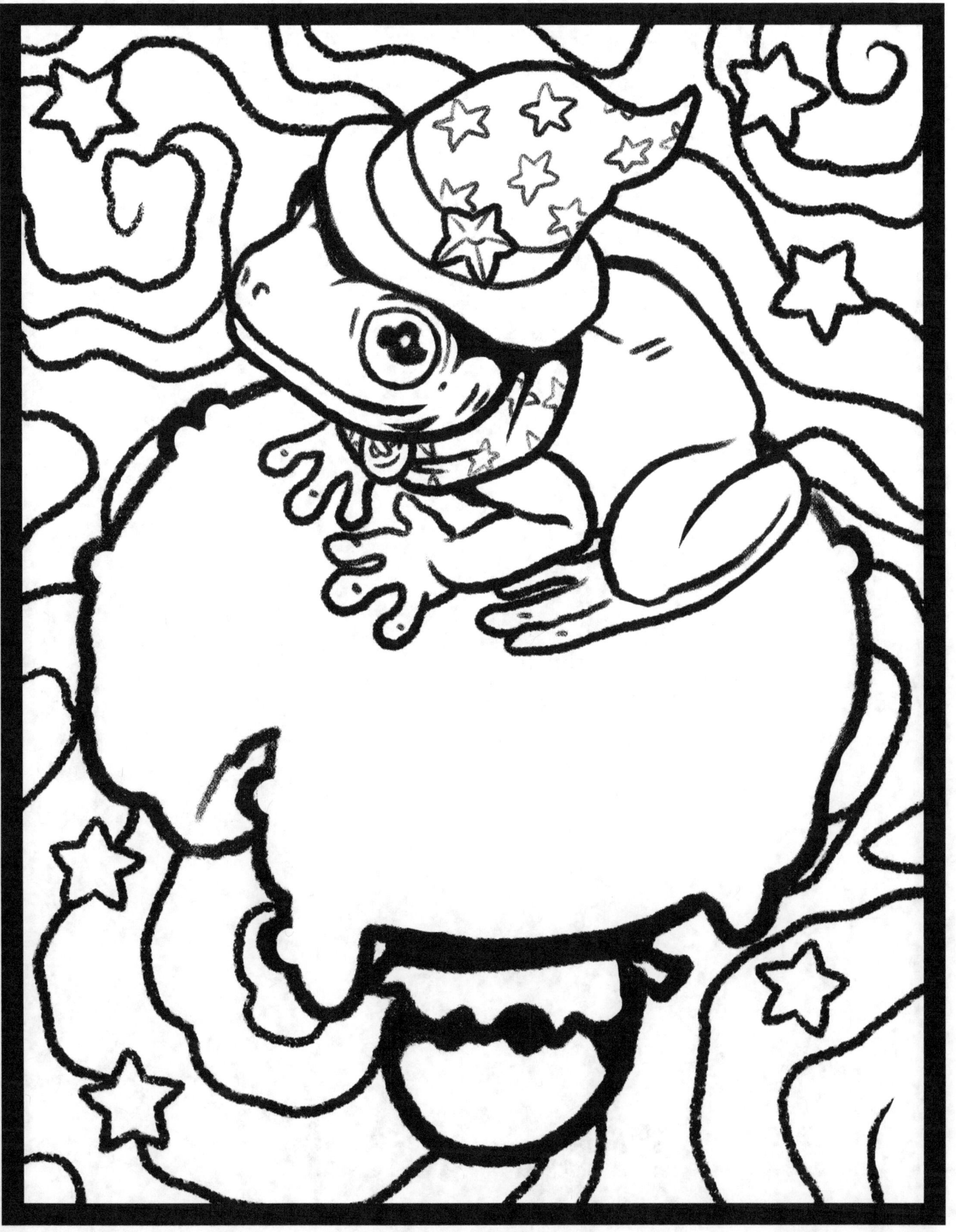

Frog Witch

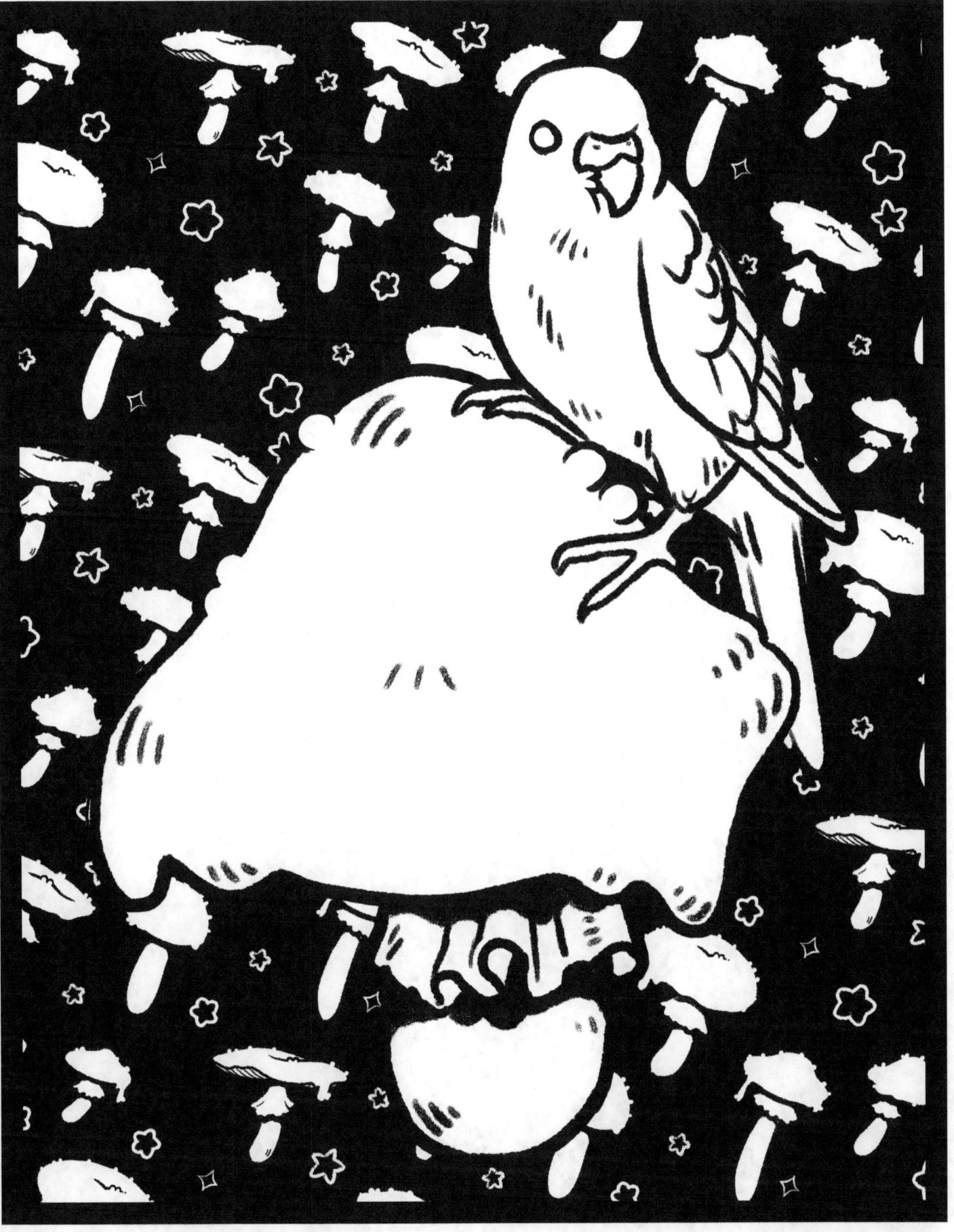

Peppy Parakeet

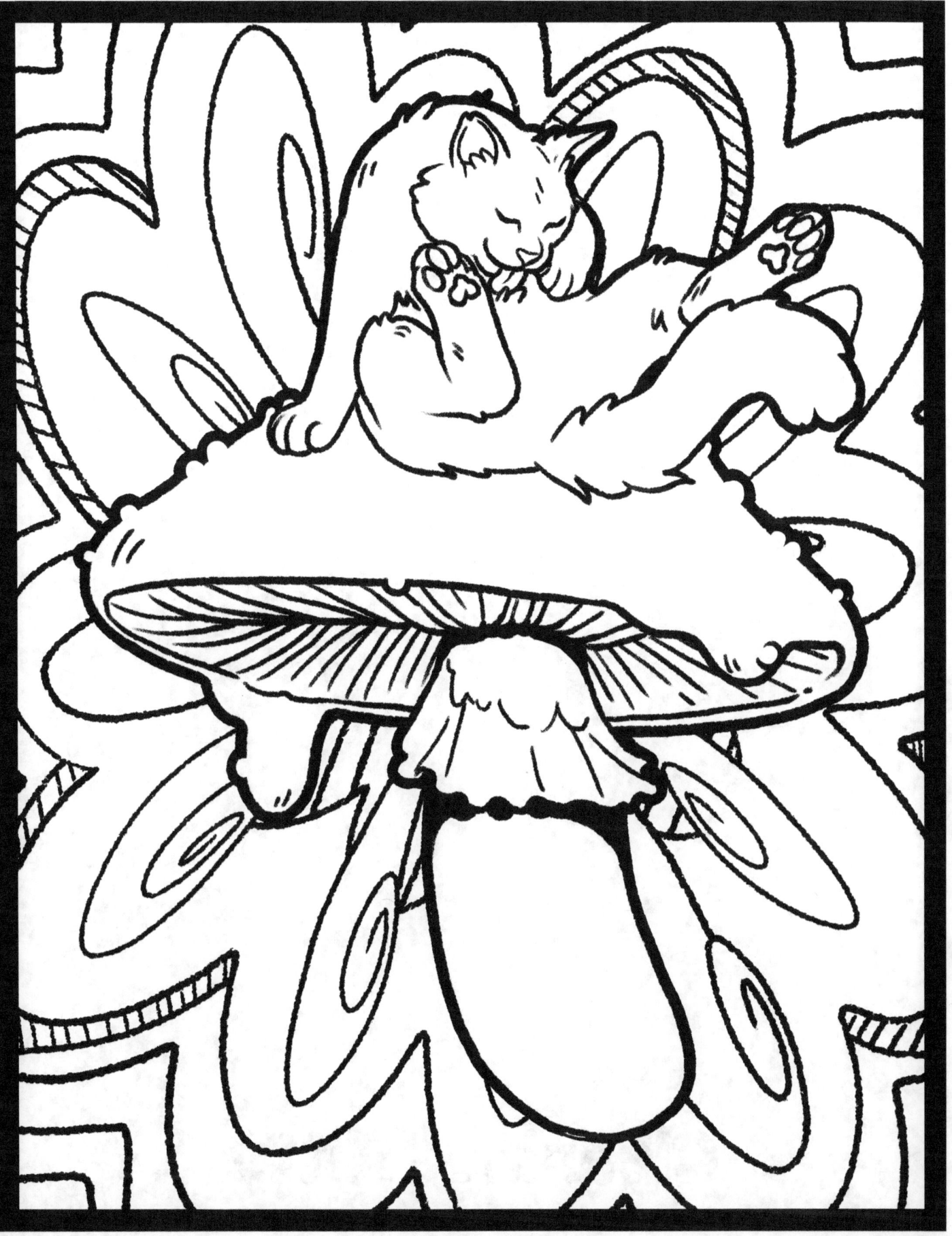

Cleaning Kitty

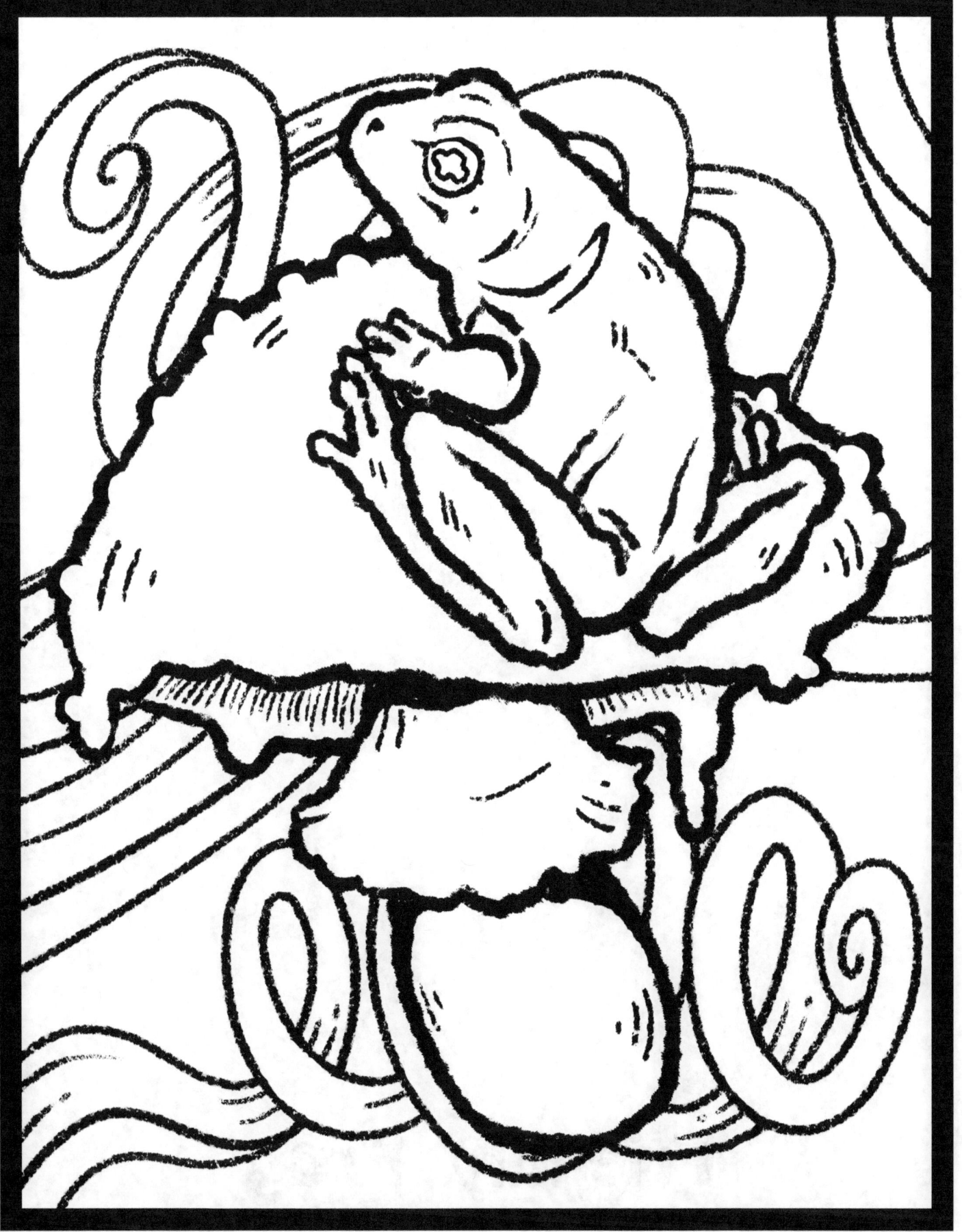

Friendly Frog

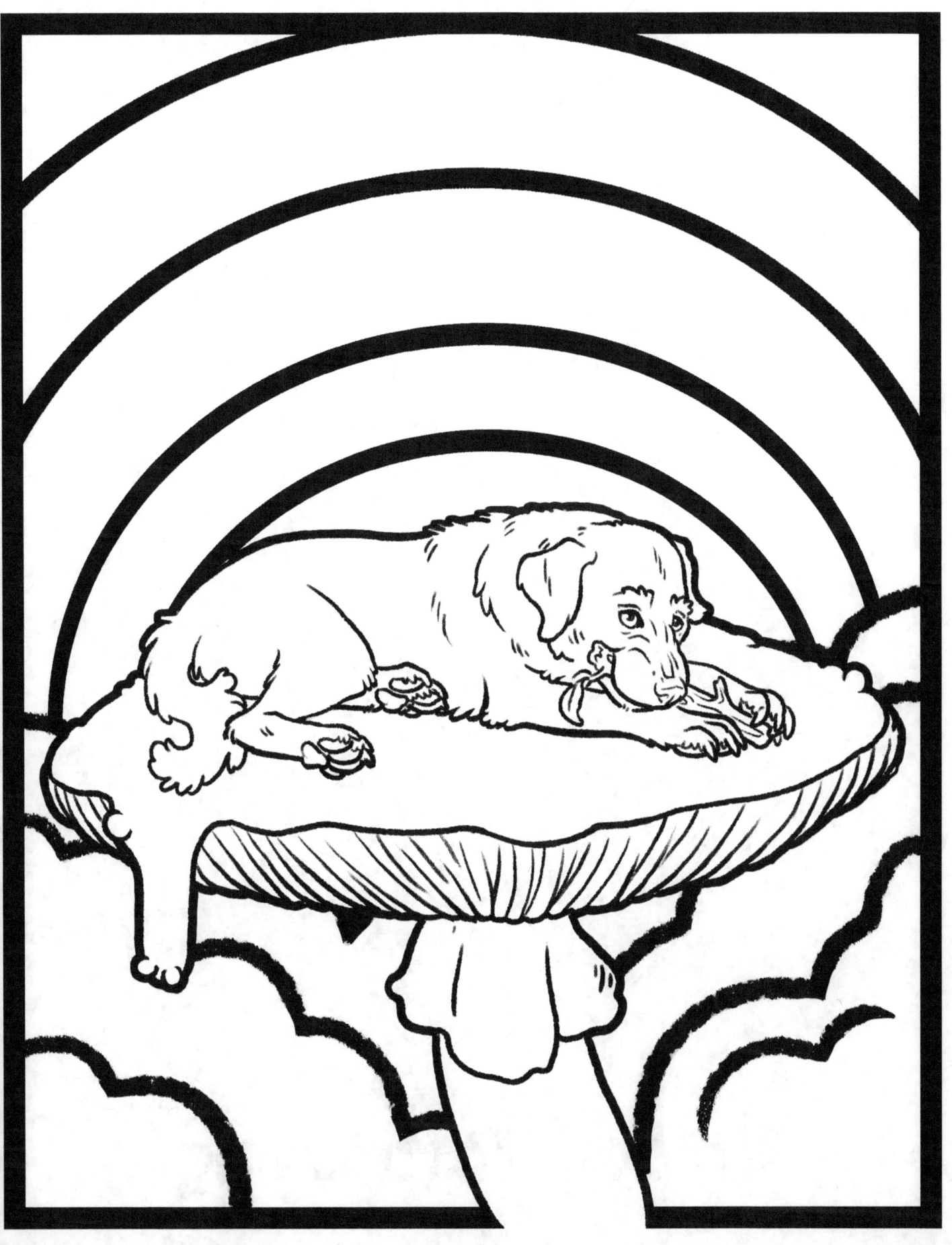

Golden Retrieving

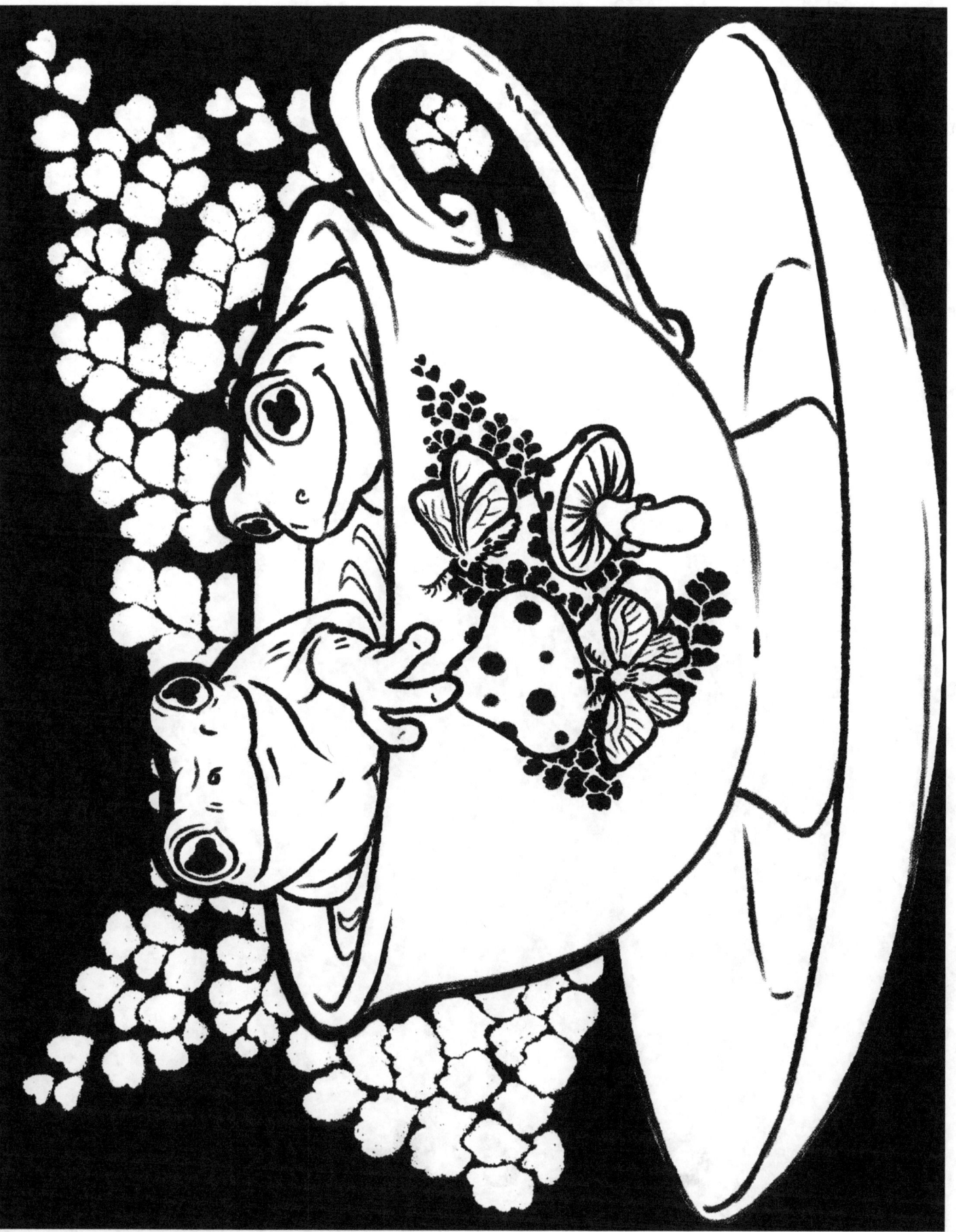

Cup 'o Frogs

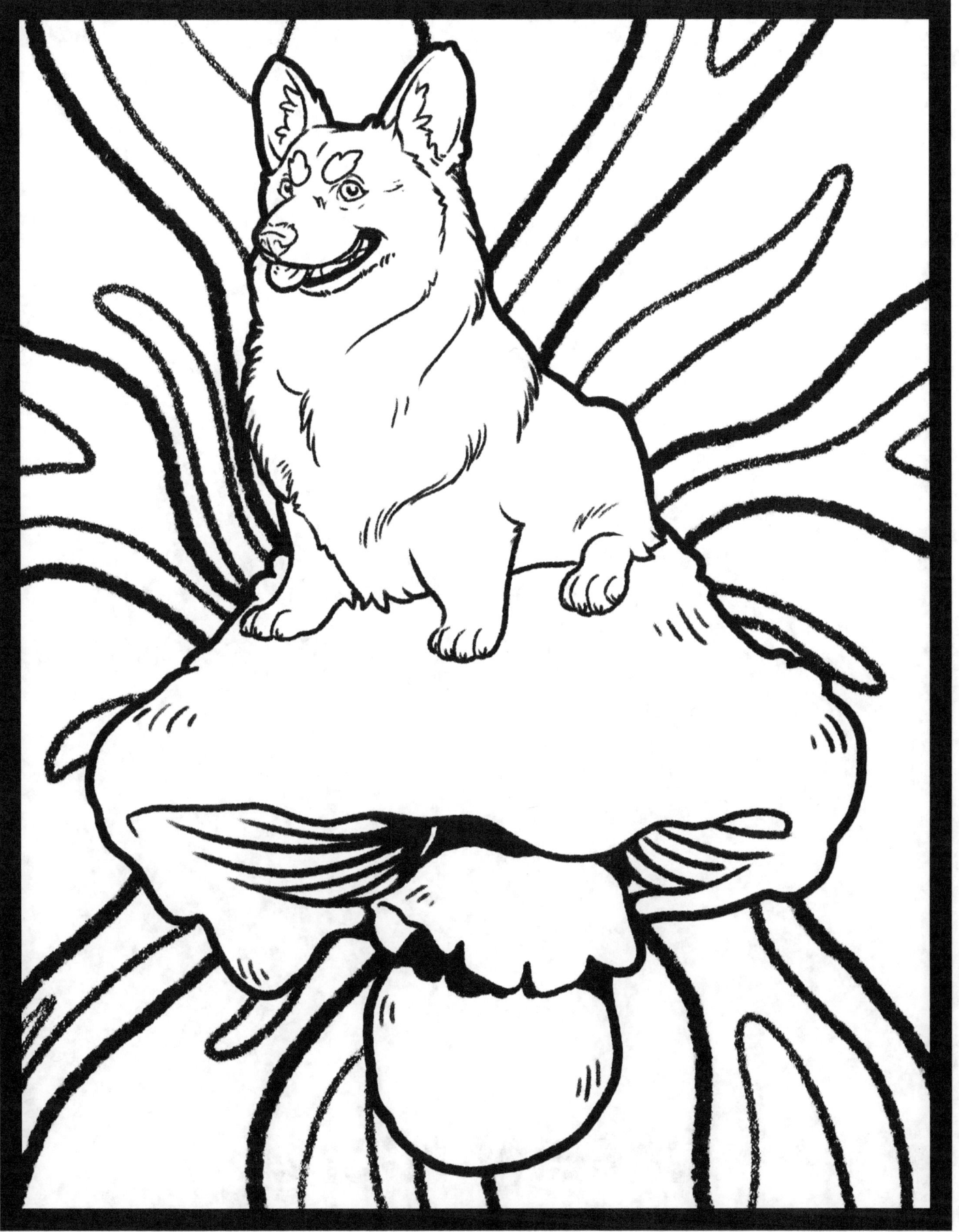

Cheery Corgi

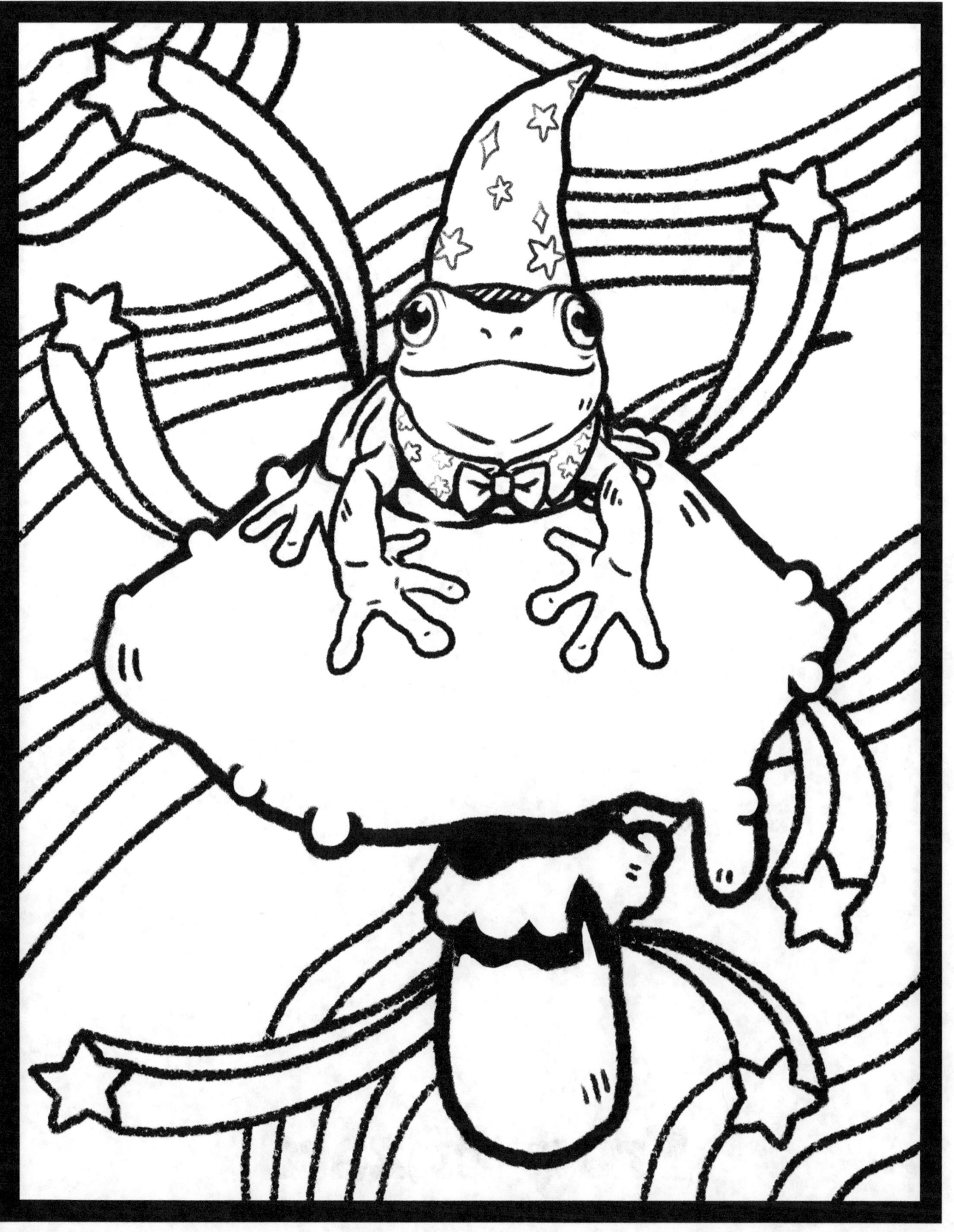

Frog Wizard

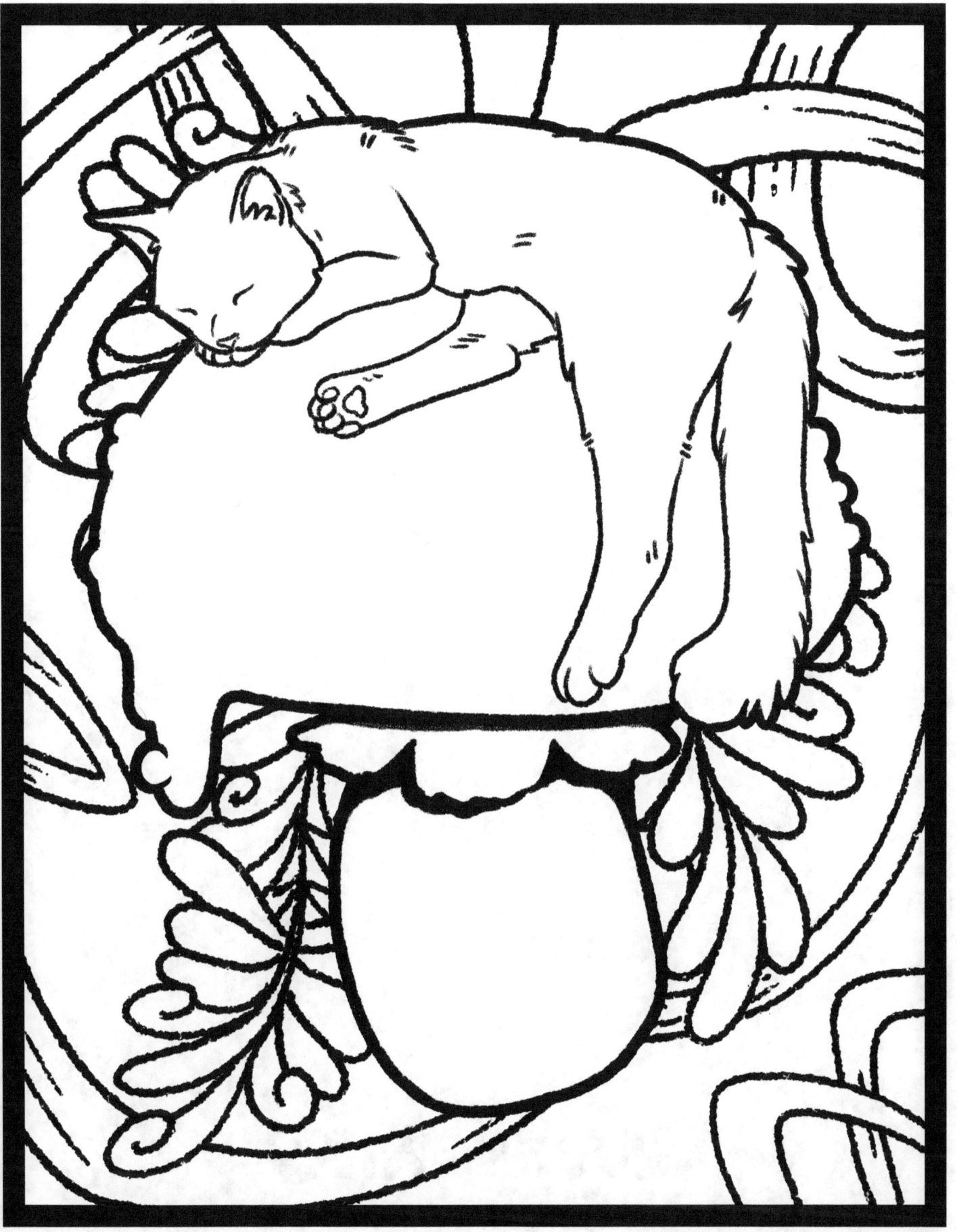

Sleepy Kitty

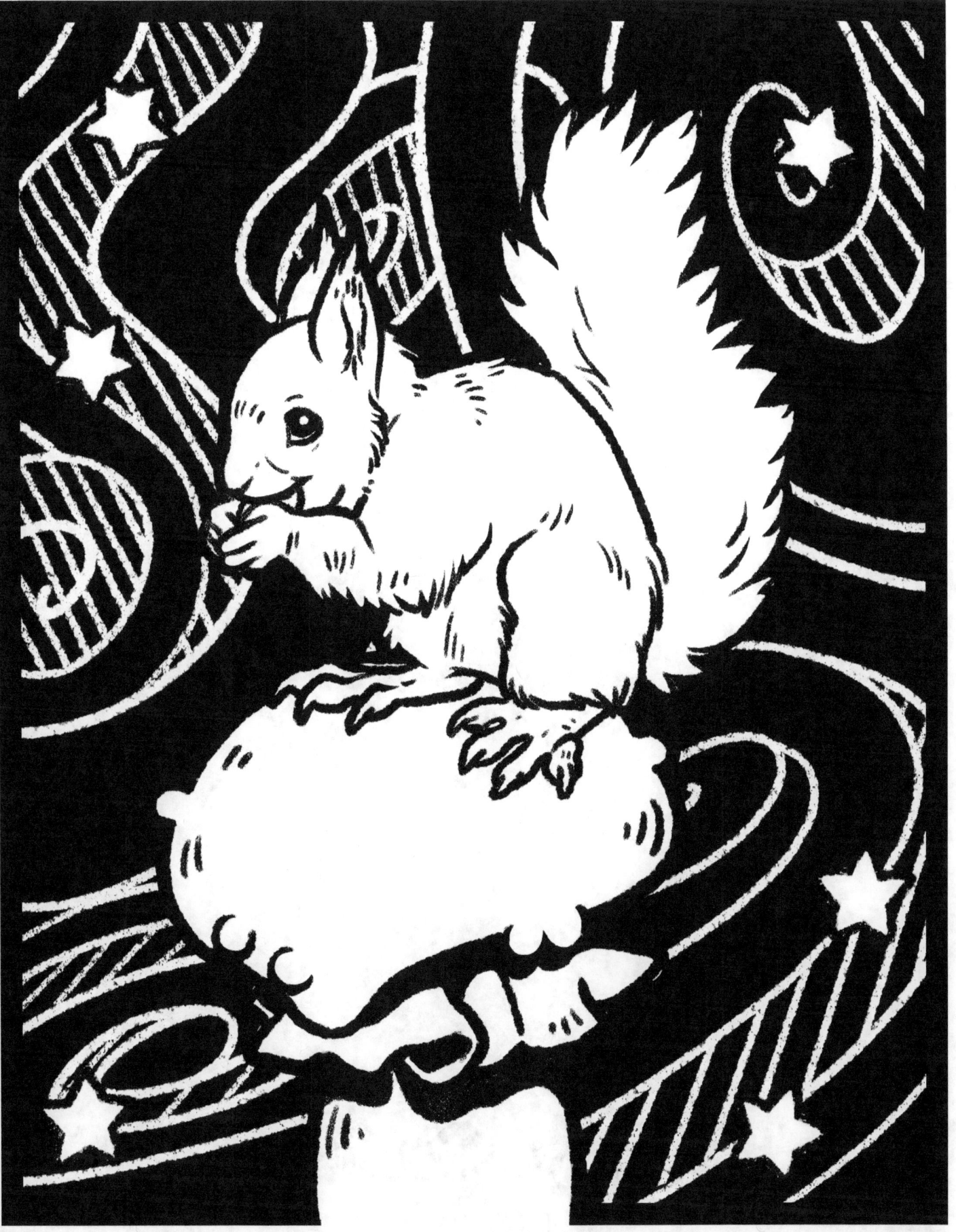

Sunny Squirrel

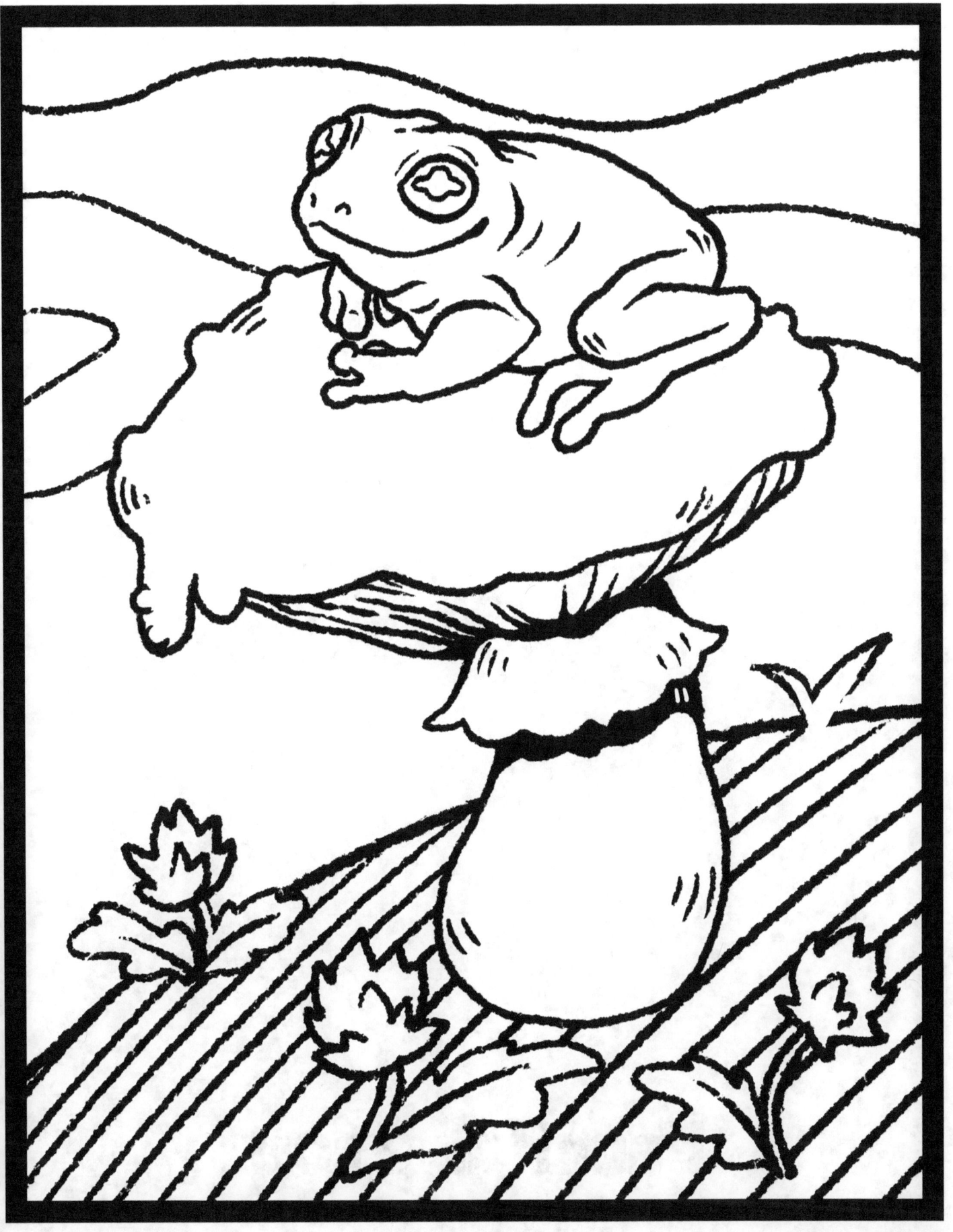

Fanciful Frog

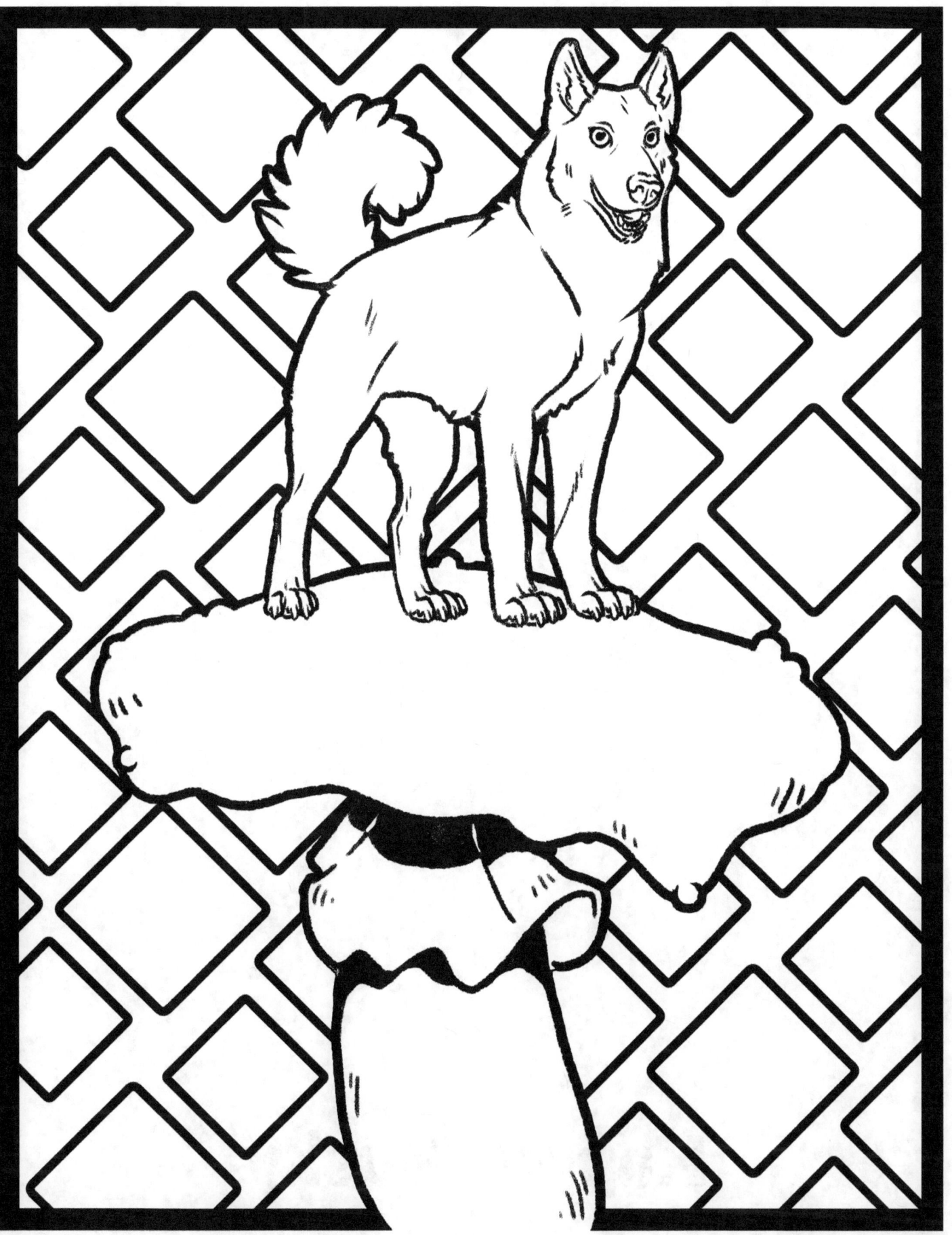

Happy Husky

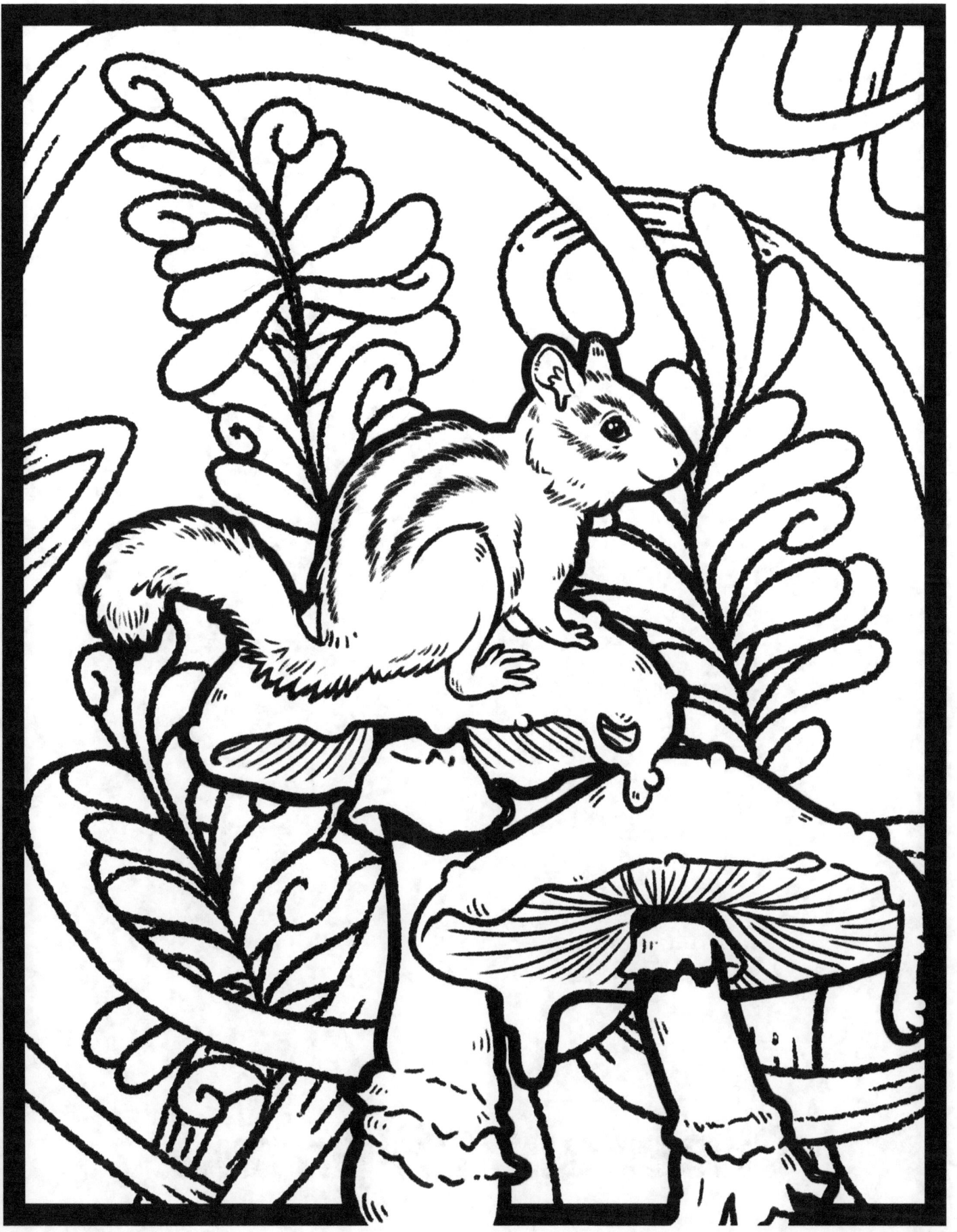

Cheerful Chipmunk

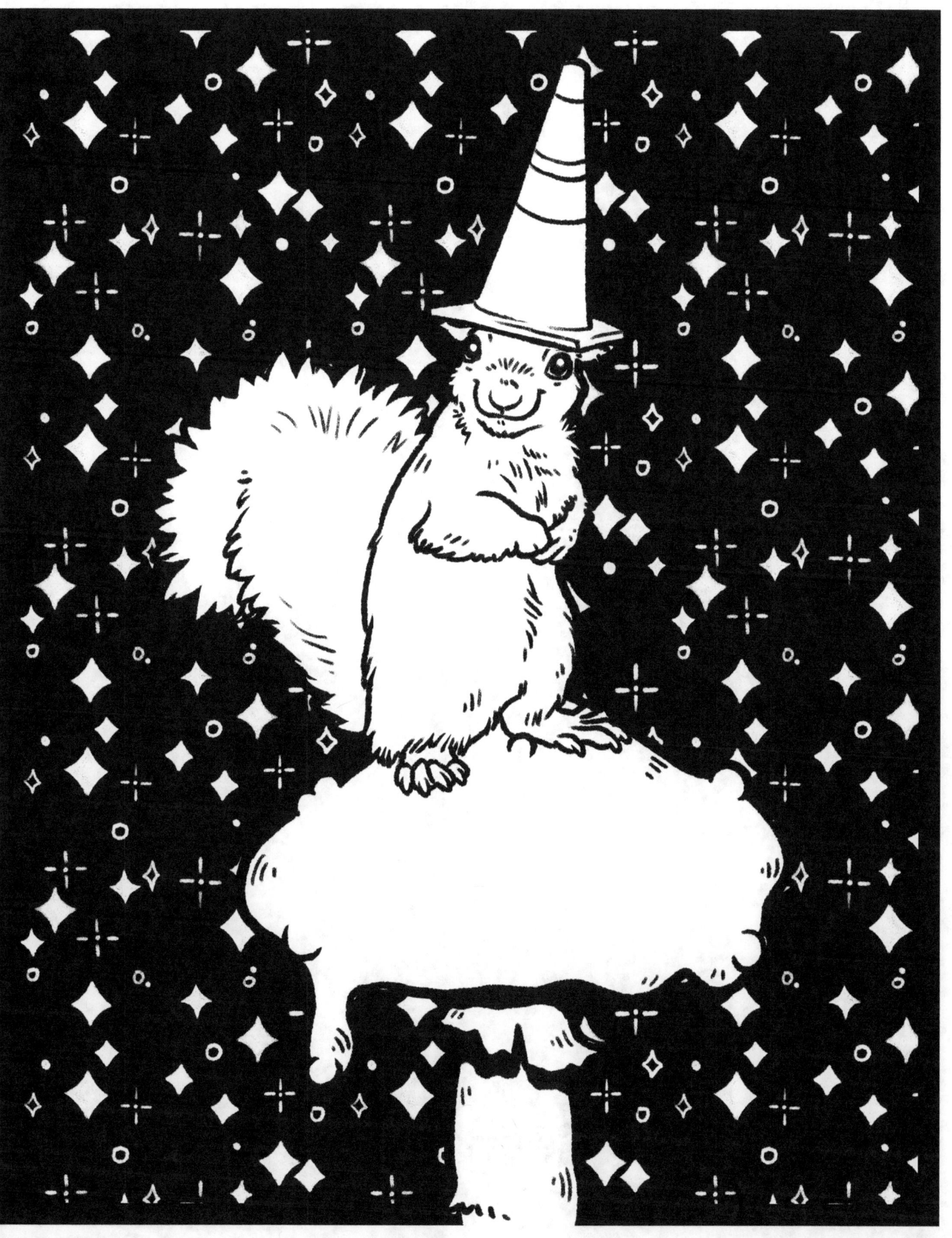

Have You Seen These Cones?

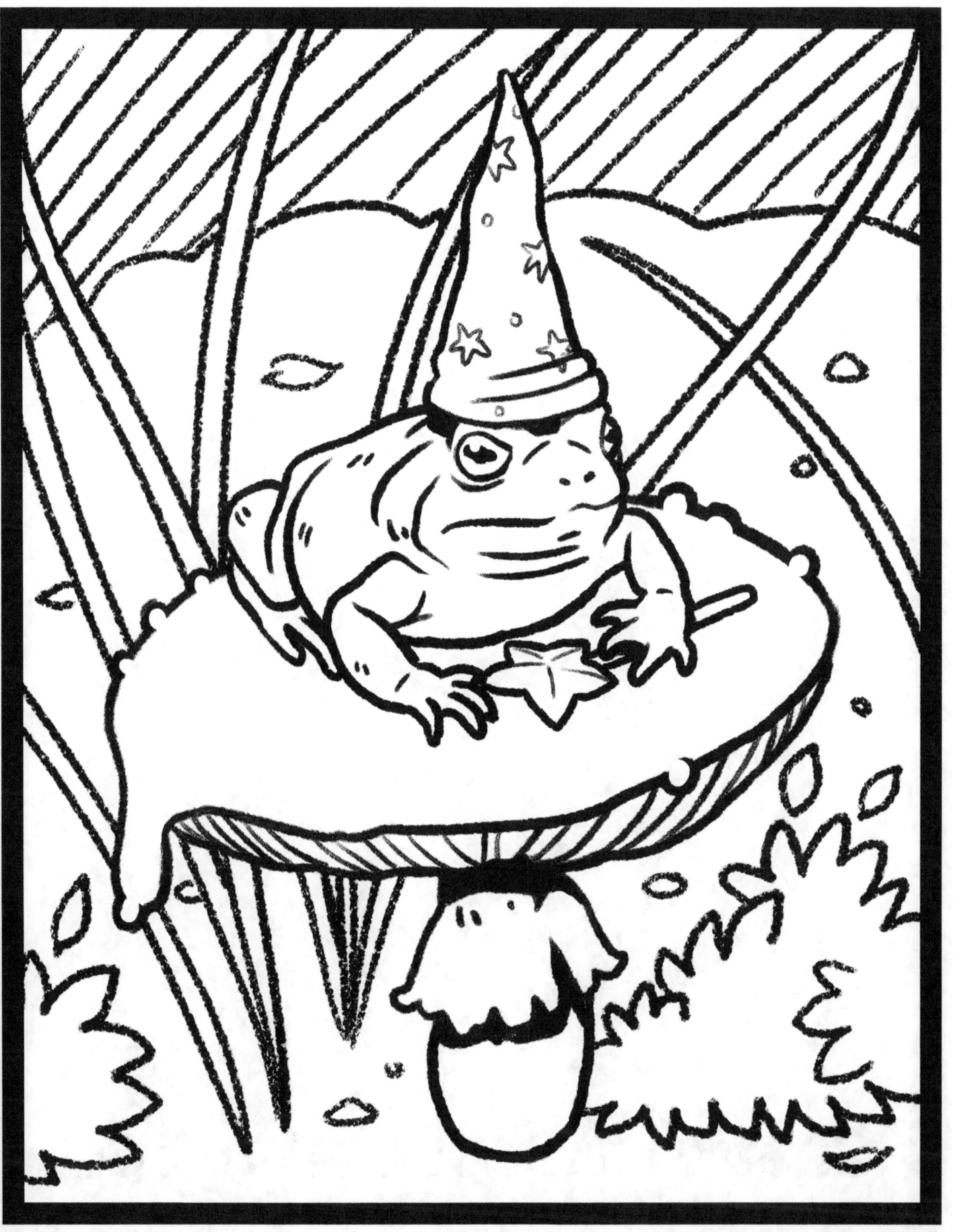

Castin' a Spell On You

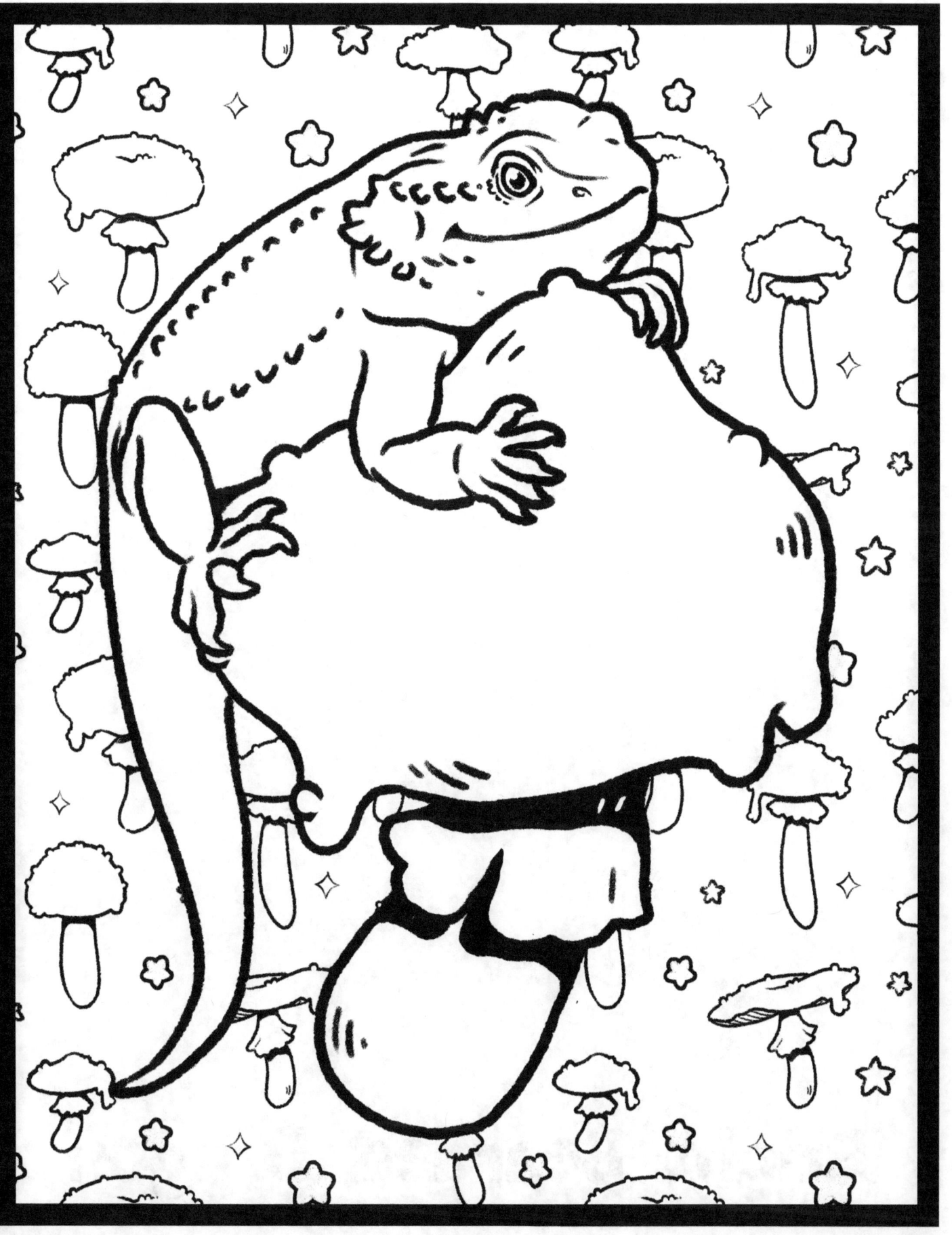

Bright Bearded Dragon

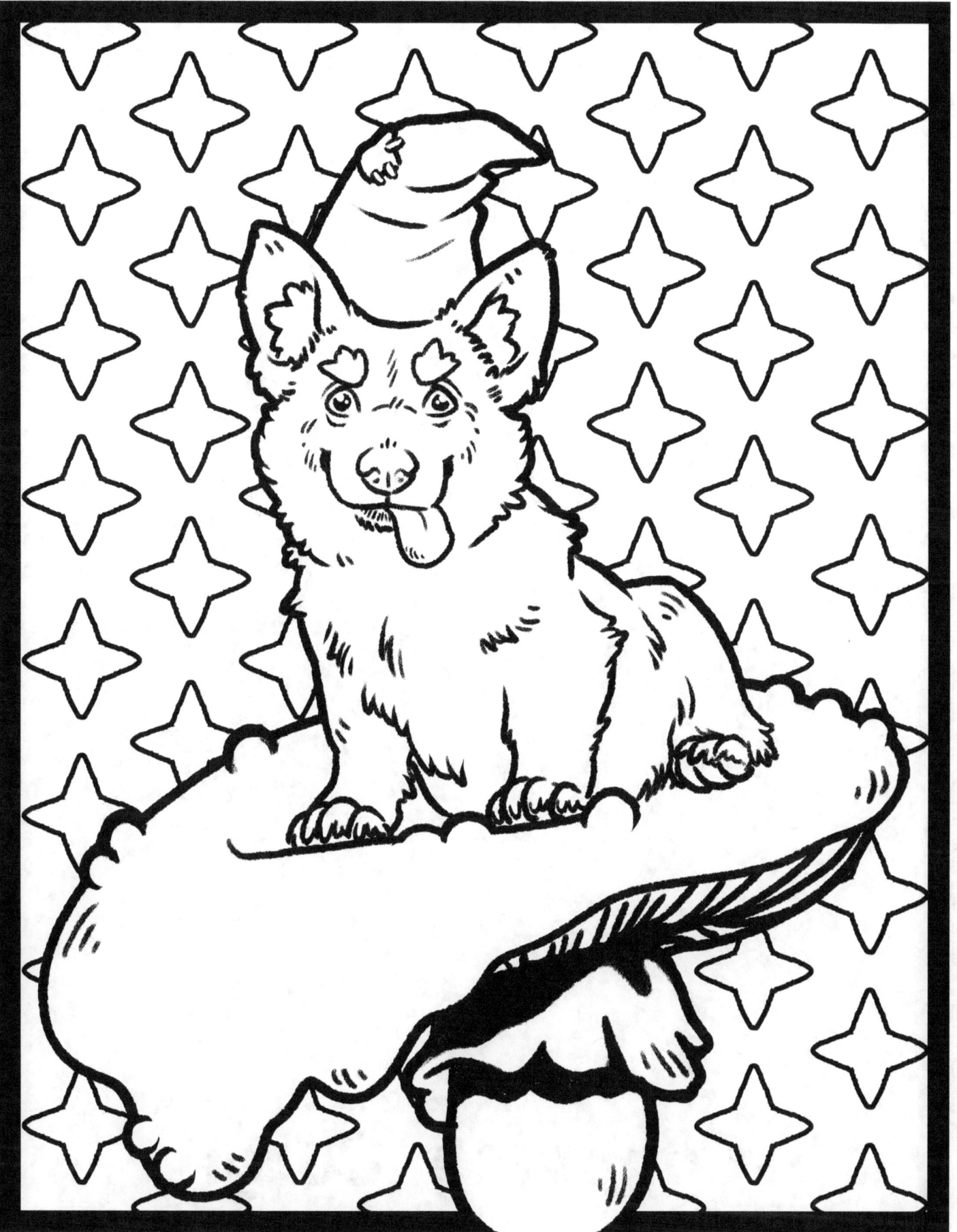

Conjuring Corgi

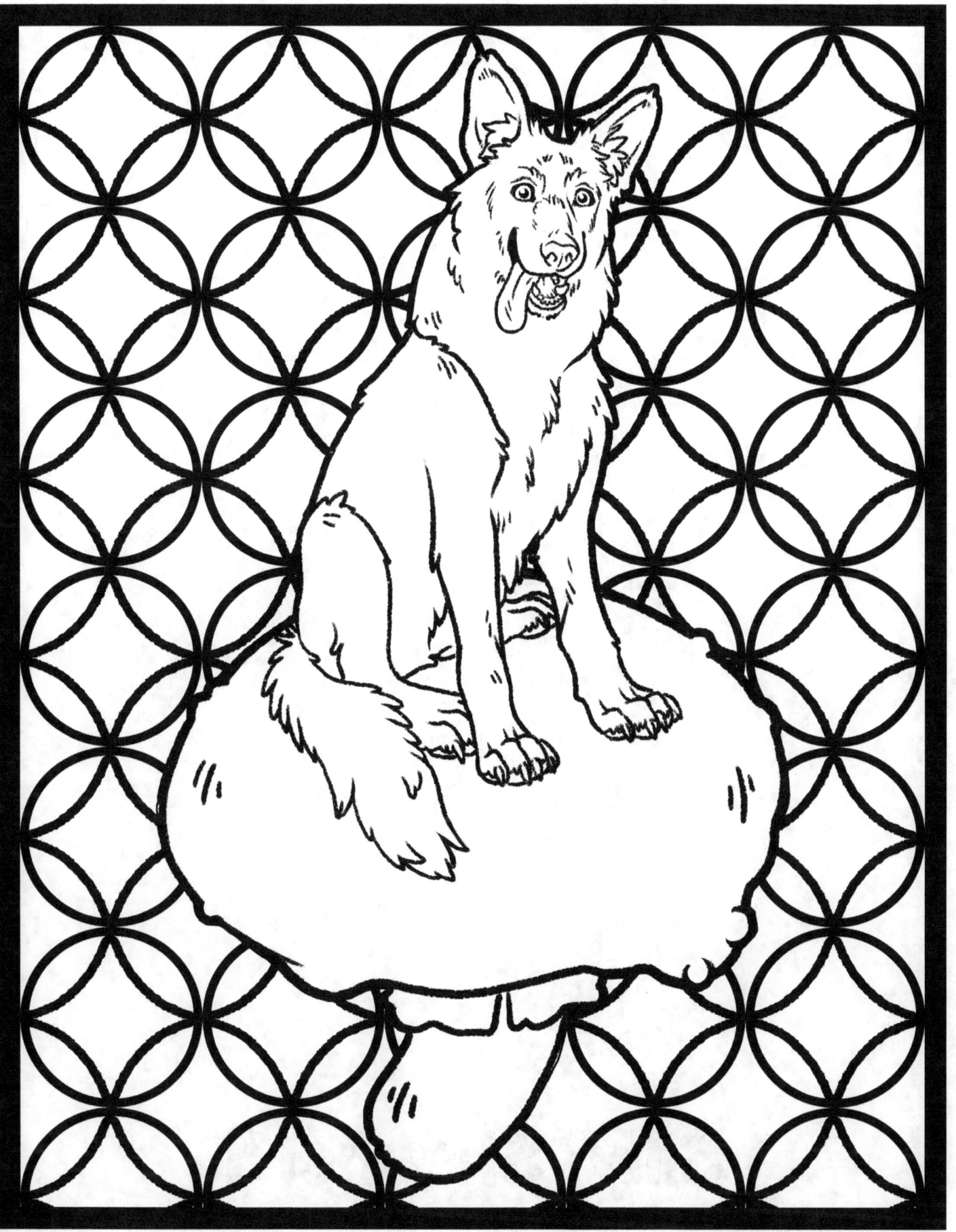

Silly Shepherd

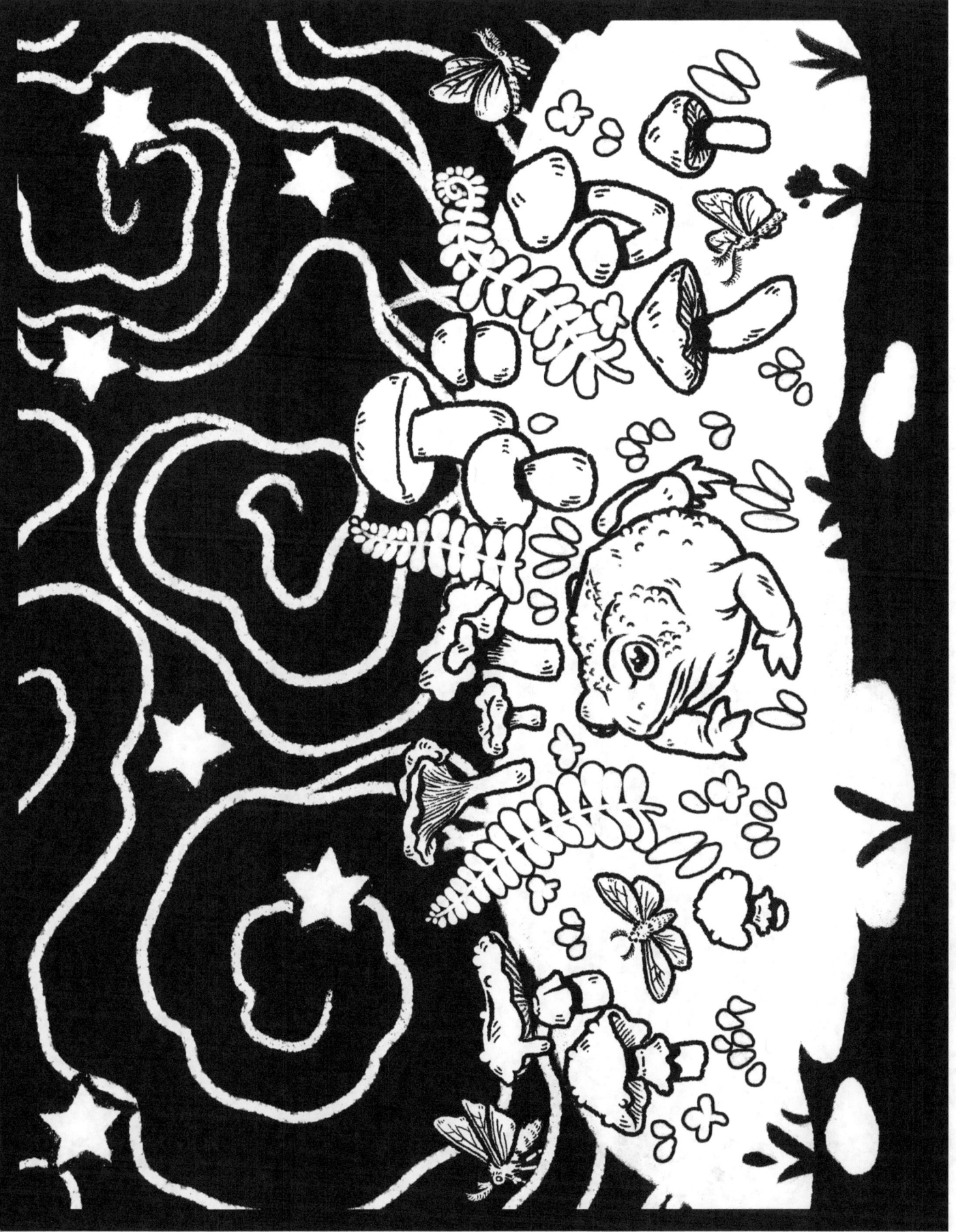

In The Garden of Shroom

TEST ART SUPPLIES HERE!

Media Test